This book is dedicated to those courageous souls who recognize that their lives could be more fulfilling, yearn to explore further, and choose to move in the direction of their dreams.

My love and eternal gratitude to Alissa and Ron, who have taught me the most important lessons.

"Follow your bliss and the universe will open doors where there were only walls."

—Joseph Campbell

Published by Another 8 Hours Publishing
A division of Another 8 Hours, Inc.
O'Fallon, IL 62269
http://www.Another8Hours.com

Library of Congress Control Number: 2011962887
Anderson, Robin

Design and typography
by Misty Wilt Graphic Design LLC
www.mistywilt.com

First Printing January, 2012
ISBN 978-0-9828585-4-7

Printed in the United States of America

JS McCarthy Printers
www.jsmccarthy.com

Back cover photo by Heidi Lynne Photography

Reclaim Your Power!

become

who

you

were

meant

to be

Robin Anderson, MS Ed, CPCC
Certified Life Coach

Table of Contents

Why This Book?

You have picked up this book because something has made you curious. Perhaps the "reclaim your power" intrigues you. Or there's that nagging feeling that you are hunting for something and yet it is too hazy to define. Still there is a pull— something is definitely calling to you. I know. I have been in your shoes.

It took me too many years to realize that my power had gotten lost in the everyday busyness of my life. I had become so good at taking care of others, constantly looking outward, that I had forgotten how to take care of myself and set aside time for reflection. I had lost the ability to say "no," and I had been shaped by others' expectations. Ultimately, I had lost myself!

Here's the story of my convoluted path to greater self-awareness and personal power. My hope is that you can learn from my experiences and more quickly identify what you really want in your life—and then for it with gusto.

I've had an interesting relationship with being the gutsy one. When I was a kid, I was always the neighborhood instigator, the daredevil. Tell me that I couldn't do something, and I'd puff up my chest, dig in my heels, and do something completely outrageous just to prove you wrong.

Somewhere along the line I lost that capacity, or perhaps I buried it because "nice girls" don't go against the grain.

Following the advice of others, I diverged from my original career path to become a teacher—a "safe" choice. Again, ignoring my true inner compass.

Eventually, I tired of teaching and began a corporate career. Tentatively, and through the mentoring of several well-placed females, I began to let my true self appear occasionally. Each appearance emboldened me and gave me back a piece of my authentic self.

I carried this emerging self into my next career, where I purposefully pushed her to soar, awakening the joy of finally being true to the real me. And I discovered my desire to coach other women so they, too, could find more personally and professionally fulfilling lives.

What crystallized my ultimate turnaround? It took a major life change, the death of my first husband, an event that so shook my world I literally had to reinvent myself and my relationship with life. And so, with baby steps, I began to re-create my own identity.

All of the small, incremental steps began to converge until I could feel my power as surely as I could feel my breath. I discovered that confidence and belief in oneself, being open to opportunities, and taking risks replenished and intensified my power. I became a force to be reckoned with, and I made things happen. But I was still missing an important piece: I was often putting my self-care at the bottom of my to-do list. And I was still relying on others for validation as well as approval of my self-image.

But progress was being made! I was at least *aware* of how I was giving away some of my power. That awareness made me realize it was not something I was willing to continue.

A few years ago I had the opportunity to retire from a job I loved but that had far too much stress associated with it. My goal was not to retire "from something" but "to something." I was a bit hazy on the "what," but I knew I would not be bored.

At this major crossroads in my life, I sought the help of a life coach. She helped me fan my inner fire, embrace audacity, and solidify my philosophy, aptly described by Dylan Thomas:

"Do not go gentle into that good night,
Old age should burn and rage at close of day;
Rage, rage against the dying of the light."

I wanted to head powerfully into my future, knowing that I still had gifts to give to the world. Once again I sought someone to help me to embrace the unknown, and courageously take the first step. Upon reflection, in the course of my life there has always been someone saying, "Yes, you can!" to every doubt I had. I have come to realize that tough girls need support, too, and smart girls ask for it!

As an audacious retirement gift to myself (my power in action), I went on a Vision Quest in the canyon lands of Utah: four solitary, fasting days, with only my camping gear, journal, and water purifier. My goal: push my limits, discover the next phase of my life, and choose how I wanted to spend my energy in the days left to me on this earth.

This was one of the toughest challenges I have ever experienced in all facets— physical, mental, and emotional. I was scared, lonely, elated, in awe, proud, energized, introspective, cleansed, and revitalized. I learned that I am much stronger than I ever gave myself credit for, that I actually enjoy taking risks, that I can push through my fears, and ultimately, that *I can do anything*. What an amazing gift!

Once I reintegrated with civilization, I set about channeling my power to realize my vision, which has become a significantly ramped up version of what I had been doing informally through most of my life: mentoring women, creating networks where there were none, and inviting women to rekindle their fire and reclaim their power. I researched the possibilities to create a framework for my mission and spent nearly eighteen months acquiring the formal training, experience and certification to give me professional credibility.

I am constantly amazed at the quality of my life now. I have new, abundant energy, I meet challenges head on, and I know I am making a difference because I am changing the world one woman at a time. I am joyously helping them re-awaken *their* inner fire, and consciously choose to live their most audacious and wildly fulfilling lives, on their terms. Not only am I living in vivid Technicolor glory, but also the gutsy, daredevil girl is back, offering a role model for other women!

Throughout my life I have had the label "role model" assigned to me, to which my response had always been, "But I'm just being me." I never really wanted to own the responsibility. However, I now willingly and joyously accept the label "Elder." My identity as an Elder combines my age, my significantly grey hair, and the hard-earned resilience and wisdom I have gained through my experiences. It is time to give back.

So, the real reason for this book is that somewhere in my life I lost myself. I happily, and often unconsciously, gave away my power. I thought that's what "good" girls do. But life's circumstances forced me to reassess who was in charge of my life. Through the examples and help from other women, and men, I began to recognize and believe in my power.

I know what it feels like to be where you are. I know that nagging feeling that something is missing—if only you could figure out what it is. My goal is to help you shortcut the awakening. I don't want you to waste as many years as I did finally figuring this out!

My message to you: you *can* rediscover your power too! It still lives inside you, even if it remains only a tiny ember. All you need is some kindling, some oxygen, and a willingness to stoke the tiny flame.

Your life's journey has carried you here based on the choices you have made along the way. Consider how much better your choices will be, and how much brighter the path will be, when you carry within yourself the flame of greater self-understanding and fulfillment.

Your power is seeking a rebirth. It's that voice that keeps repeating, "Is this all there is to my life?" You've already taken the first step! You are becoming more open to the possibilities and you are ready to listen deeply to your most authentic inner voice. You have begun to discover the most astounding gifts – just awaiting you!

Let the new leg of your journey begin!

Planning Your Journey

"It is good to have an end to journey toward; but it is the journey that matters, in the end." —Ursula K. LeGuin

You are seeking a change, and change can sometimes be unsettling. I understand. My goal is to provide a safe environment for your journey.

I have designed this book in a user-friendly workbook style, purposefully using a conversational manner with heavy emphasis on encouragement. Each chapter contains a discussion of the topic followed by a series of exercises in self-discovery. These powerful questions will help you create an awareness of where and how you have stifled your power and identify where you are playing small. Use the space provided to reflect on who you are down deep inside and what you truly want in your life. You also may want to make use of a personal journal to expand on the exercises, capture ideas or personal learning, and note insights. This is about your growth, so do it your way!

You will find In Real Life anecdotes from my life and the lives of my clients. I hope these examples will reinforce that you are not alone in your feelings, desires, worries, dreams, fears, and longings.

Many chapters end with a Meditation Moment. These pauses will allow you to more fully integrate your learnings and "a-ha's." I recommend that you spend a minimum of ten minutes on the specified exercise. In reality your experience with meditation may vary. If you are new to meditation, you may want to meditate in shorter periods across several sessions until you become more comfortable with longer periods. If you currently have a meditation practice, you may want to extend the Meditation Moment and mine its richness. Bottom line: it's important that you spend dedicated time to fully be with your discoveries and desires. It is far too easy to just check off each exercise and move to the next. Use these opportunities to observe and deepen your learning and to work through your challenges so you can remove the barriers.

I highly recommend that you progress from front to back—building awareness, refining what you want in your life, and developing the tools to keep you in motion on this personal journey. And for those of you who enjoy looking at the ending of a book before you begin reading, just know that each chapter builds on its predecessor. The early chapters will establish a firm foundation, and then, layer upon layer, you will refine your vision and strengthen your resolve so that you can clarify your path to a more fulfilling life. You will create a vision so powerful, so juicy, and so irresistible, that you absolutely must have it!

If my intention is effective, you are going to want to leap into action. Of course, you want action! You have come to this book looking for a way to make changes in your life. You may begin to think, "So, let's get on with it! " This attitude will certainly kick start your journey. And yet, so many of us just pile more and more onto our to-do list. Then each "to-do" becomes less important. Action alone is not sustainable for the long haul.

So your journey needs to involve a blend of action and being. Notice the *and* in that sentence. Your actions must be anchored to the new way you are being in the world. By reflecting on where you are now and where you are heading, you can better nourish your resolve to stay in action. There is great benefit in slowing down so that you can fully appreciate your growth and make adjustments to your path. The most amazing gift arrives once you consciously choose to change: previously unimaginable opportunities appear! Your horizons expand. Possibilities become unlimited.

So my recommendation is that you pace yourself. Take time to savor your learning for it will guide you to your next action. The journey of self-discovery cannot be hurried. You will need time to be with who you are becoming and to be fully present with any emotions or feelings that may arise. You may discover things about yourself that have long been buried and are now crying to be heard. Recognizing and accepting these revelations may require time. Only you know when it is right to move to the next step in the process of personal change.

This is not a once-and-done workbook. Wherever you are on your journey, the exercises can be used again and again to help you to add more audacity and fulfillment to your life. What an exciting path lies ahead!

It's hard to fight an enemy who has outposts in your head.

—Sally Kempton

This Is No Way to Go through Life!

In my coaching practice I often ask women where and when they give away their power, and to whom. Too often they confide that they let others define them, whether it is their self-worth, their body image, or whose opinion "counts." And while they so willingly give their power to others, these women often sabotage themselves by heeding the advice of their own inner critic. This does not make for a powerful, satisfying situation. Where is the true, authentic voice of each of these women? Too often they allow their voice to be limited by others or they freely give away their power. These behaviors often lead to feelings of resentment, lack of fulfillment and a sense of being stuck.

Let's face it—right now you're probably spending much of your precious time nurturing others, thinking about others, and being responsible for others. It's an "other" world, and you're the main character.

Oh sure, on any given day you don't mind this role. After all, you play it so well. But then there are those days when your inner fire is burning low, you've lost your way, and all it takes is one little thing—a misplaced cell phone, a forgotten appointment, a crabby co-worker—to throw things into a complete tailspin, leaving you frenzied and ready to explode.

It's those days that are becoming a bit too frequent lately, and you're starting to think a little harder about what your life means. There's that vague feeling that something is missing—the unnamed beckoning to feel more *deliciousness* in your life. You're tired of the same-old, same-old every day, over and over. Auto-pilot is so… unfulfilling.

Well, I have something to say to you: This is no way to go through your life!

I can hear the "Yes, buts…" starting to fill the air. Your inner critic's voice gets louder and louder the more you think about making any changes. It's the voice that says, "If you do this, you will be

REJECTED,
    laughed at,
        poor,
            WRONG,
                all alone,
                    embarrassed,
DISAPPOINTING SOMEONE,
          found out,
              selfish,
                  and on, and on, and on."

Ah, the voice of your inner critic. Oh, yeah, that voice you know so well. For now, find a gentle way to set aside this all-too-familiar companion. We will deal with it later. I promise.

What if your life could be different? What if you could joyously greet each day and feel bursting with energy and joy? What if your life felt more in tune and harmonious? What if you could feel more empowered and less at the mercy of circumstances?

Possibilities – freedom – creativity – adventure – purpose: these gifts are just waiting for you. Your curiosity and longing have brought you here. You've already taken the first step!

You know you want a change. Right now it may be a tiny fleeting thought. Or, you may have an idea of where you want to be. Maybe you've had a glimpse of what might be different, but "if only" holds you back.

Whatever your starting point, this book is designed to help you on your journey. My job is to pose thought-provoking questions, offer reflective opportunities, and get you into action. Your job is to be willing to explore and to be open and receptive.

This means moving beyond the "should's" in your life, quieting your inner critic and setting aside any presumptions. This is your opportunity to redefine your life, *on your terms*, by identifying what *you* really want. This is about putting yourself back into the driver's seat, setting your course, and navigating from a place of power. This is about identifying your priorities and values, and building the confidence to be proactive rather than reactive. This is about honoring yourself. This is about realizing your dreams. Yes, you really do have the power to make them happen!

Giving Away Your Power

"Your time is limited, so don't waste it living someone else's life." –Steve Jobs

From personal experience and working with my coaching clients, I have observed a recurring theme: not recognizing or giving away personal power. This often shows up as a lack of self-confidence, allowing "others" to make all of the decisions, "going along to get along," getting caught up in other people's drama, not standing up for personal beliefs, discounting personal skills and abilities, being the "nice girl," or doing anything not to appear "selfish."

All of these situations are the direct result of giving away your personal power. Bottom line? This means *letting others determine what you think, feel, and believe*, and how you behave.

These behaviors crowd out and overwhelm your sense of self, your authenticity, and your true inner voice. In essence you're choosing to let others run your life!

There is a key thing to remember in all of these situations: you are making a choice! You are choosing, most often unconsciously, to relinquish your power. Over time you begin to feel resentment. You've been taken advantage of and intimidated. You feel unseen and unheard. You begin to live life small. Your voice becomes softer, less noticeable. The real you fades.

> *The key thing to remember: in all of these situations you are making a choice! You are choosing, most often unconsciously, to relinquish your power.*

So, what's going on here?

Most often, we let our sense of self-worth be defined by someone other than ourselves. The mass media influences how we feel about our weight, the

Make a conscious choice to reawaken your innate spark by identifying your dreams, and you

wrinkles we have, or the strands of grey hair that begin to appear. We're too short, too tall, too fat, too thin, too busy, not busy enough, too selfish, and on, and on, and on. We let other people—family, friends, the boss, co-workers, and more—be the mirror that reflects how we think and feel about ourselves. We seek approval and validation from outside of ourselves.

Or perhaps, we are fearful of confrontation. Sometimes we value "peace at any price." We don't want to cause trouble or disrupt the status quo. We "go along, to get along." On the surface everything may appear peaceful, but inside we feel depleted, maybe even angry and resentful, because we so willingly sacrifice our internal peace for the sake of keeping everyone happy and everything on an even keel—for others but not ourselves. Or we let others intimidate or overwhelm us, bullying us into submission. Or we have taken to heart someone else's belief that we must always be the "good girl" who doesn't shake up things, who readily assumes the cultural mold.

Maybe self-doubt steps in. Thoughts like, "Who am I to think that I really can do this?" Or, "I only have (level of education, experience, fill-in-the-blank), so they won't want me." We allow ourselves to reject any change before someone can turn us down. Personal amnesia prevents us from remembering what we are good at, what we really want in our lives, and what we truly believe. We are the ones who keep ourselves from saying *yes* to living large!

We try to take care of everyone at the cost of taking care of ourselves.

All of these are choices we make. These are habits and behaviors that have become ingrained in our very being. We have chosen to let others define us and how we

ife purpose, and beginning to believe that you can have your most audacious and wildly fulfilling life.

appear in the world. And all of these choices come with a hefty personal price.

But here's the thing about choice: there are *always* options leading to action. Quite literally, to choose means to select after consideration. We can choose to do or believe something, or not. If something is no longer serving us—if we want back our power—we can choose to reclaim it!

> *We can choose to do or believe something, **or not.***

Lighting Your Fire

"Do you really want to look back on your life and see how wonderful it could have been had you not been afraid to live it?" –Caroline Myss

I thought for quite some time about a metaphor that fully captures my message. Then it dawned on me that I want to help women recognize that *they already have power*, although it currently may be just a tiny ember or even a faint glow. Yet once this spark is rediscovered and consciously tended to over time, it can burst into a glorious, primal, blazing fire, something very visible and a force to be reckoned with by all who observe it. It becomes an inner glow and guiding light on the path to self-fulfillment.

You are born with an ember of power. It is a gift, and it does have strings attached: tend it and it grows ever stronger, ignore it or give it away and it diminishes. It is your choice. As with any fire, if you tend it, it will grow into a blaze lighting your way as you make your mark on the world, fulfilling your potential and your life's purpose. Ignore it and it will diminish, becoming just the faintest spark, barely visible to the eye, perhaps only a memory. Your life then becomes ho-hum, and you begin to feel stuck and without much energy.

Good news! You can make a conscious choice to reawaken your innate spark by identifying your dreams, and your life purpose, and beginning to believe that you *can* have your most audacious and wildly fulfilling life. By adding small bits and pieces of tinder—identifying what you truly want and why it is important to you—you can begin to fuel your spark.

By gently adding extra oxygen, the struggling flame can be coaxed to grow stronger. Your oxygen comes in the form of self-care, affirmations, and your support network giving you the strength to keep going. It is vitally important to keep this steady stream of oxygen feeding the spark. It's so easy for the flame to falter.

As your fire grows, so do your confidence, your sense of direction, and the "rightness" of your decisions.

As your fire grows, so do your confidence, your sense of direction, and the "rightness" of your decisions. It suddenly becomes very important to keep this fire burning ever brighter, providing warmth and a sense of well being. So you gather firewood—a renewed sense of purpose, an abundance of possibilities, even larger, previously unthinkable dreams—to sustain your fire. You begin to notice that you are quite enjoying yourself! You recognize that you have the ability to see much farther into the darkness and that the things that go bump in the night don't appear so fearful.

> *You have made this happen.*
> *You are the caretaker of your flame.*
> *You have the* **POWER!**

And, then, the "yes buts…" begin to rustle. "You're only going to be disappointed." "This is not what you're *supposed* to be doing." "Why bother, nothing will really change."

As your fire grows, so do your confidence, your sense of direction, and the "brightness" of your decisions.

Your inner critic begins to throw water on your emerging flame. You've had the audacity to disturb the comfort zone! So, you fall back on old habits and begin to second-guess yourself. You wonder why you ever considered making your flame grow bigger and brighter. "It was just a foolish daydream, wasn't it?"

Or the voices of others begin to blow at hurricane strength, trying to get your attention and squelch your fire. "You're changing things!" "You're not meeting my expectations!" "Why are you being so *selfish*?"

If you're not paying attention, the fire may die down or return to a tiny ember! And yet in the back of your mind, you keep hearing, "Yes, and, what about me? When is it time for me?"

Lighting your fire is only half the battle. How you build your fire—the pace with which you add fuel, how you arrange the structures to support its growth, how you deal with obstacles—will directly affect how long your fire will continue burning and the amount of heat and light it will provide.

An ember doesn't suddenly burst into a roaring fire; so, too, your journey will start slowly, maybe even tentatively. Yet, as you begin to nurture the spark, fanning the flame, gradually adding possibilities and dreams, and rearranging your support structures to reinforce the heat you are building, you will begin to witness your spark slowly and steadily growing. And, as your fire grows ever brighter and stronger, it will cast significantly greater light on your journey's path, allowing you to walk more confidently while illuminating unimagined possibilities ahead of you. And the world will open its arms to joyously greet the true, authentic, powerful you.

"If you don't know where you're going, you'll end up some place else."

—Yogi Berra

What's Your Current Reality?

You know you are tired of the same-old, same-old. You are stuck on how to break free. Perhaps you have some thoughts about who you want to be. Maybe you've had some insight as to what you might change, but "if only" nips at your heels.

No matter where you are now, this workbook was created to give you a kick in the pants to get you moving on your journey. My job is to heighten your awareness of what you truly want in your life. I promise to jolt your complacency and shake up your comfort zone by asking thought-provoking questions. Hopefully they will cause you to step back and reflect on the choices you are making. I will offer opportunities to shift your perspective and consider other options. Most importantly, I will strive to get you into action, so you will begin the journey to create the changes you are seeking.

Your job is to be willing to explore and to be open and receptive. This means ignoring the "should's" in your life, quieting your inner critic, and setting aside any presumptions. This is your opportunity to redefine your life, on your terms by identifying what you really want. This is about identifying your priorities and values, and building the confidence to be proactive rather than reactive. This is about honoring yourself. This is about realizing your dreams. Yes, you do have the power to make them happen.

In my coaching work, I use broad categories that reflect aspects of a whole life. How you define each segment will be highly individualized. Where you decide to focus first will be your choice. But keep in mind this maxim: how you show up in one area of your life is how you show up in all areas of your life. If you are lacking power in one area, odds are you are lacking power in other areas, too. And the good news is that as you begin to regain power in one area, you will begin to notice more power in the other areas of your life!

The first exercise will help you to recognize where you currently give away your power, to whom, and why. Creating an awareness of *what is* will help you determine where you can start to make changes. And, you do want to make changes, right?

Think of this exercise as clearing the space to make room for your spark to grow. As with building a fire, you need to remove the brush, the undergrowth, the remnants of dead branches and leaves. Later you will be adding small bits and pieces of tinder— identifying what you truly want and why it is important to you—so you can begin to fuel your spark.

Identifying Your Power Leaks

We are going to examine your entire life to help you see the bigger picture, and identify any patterns that may emerge The decisions we make are interconnected, with effects extending unseen in all directions. You don't compartmentalize your life—you just go about living it—so we are going to look into every nook and cranny to shine a light on the here-and-now, your reality. Your goal is to create an awareness of the Now so you can better envision where you want to be in the future. Later you will identify your personal values which will help you consciously move into the future you desire, and identify any obstacles that may interfere with your forward motion.

You will examine the following eight major segments of your life:

- ➢ Physical Well-being
- ➢ Rejuvenation
- ➢ Close Relationships
- ➢ Love Life
- ➢ Personal Growth
- ➢ Physical Surroundings
- ➢ Work
- ➢ Money

The definition of these terms is unique to you. I invite you to describe what they mean to you, in your life. Remember, this is all about you and what you truly want. The more you can specifically describe the terms, the more deeply you will come to know yourself and the choices you are making.

For each area, write your description of what the term means to you. Then reflect on how you relinquish your power, to whom, and why you do so.

Physical Well-being

This area might include your physical health and strength, self-image, weight, illness, etc.

I define physical well-being as

I give away my power to

when I

because

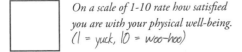

On a scale of 1-10 rate how satisfied you are with your physical well-being.
(1 = yuck, 10 = woo-hoo)

Rejuvenation

This area might include how you recharge your batteries, creative expression, physical activities, the amount of laughter in your life, etc.

I define rejuvenation as

I give away my power to

when I

because

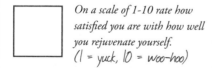

On a scale of 1-10 rate how
satisfied you are with how well
you rejuvenate yourself.
(1 = yuck, 10 = woo-hoo)

Close Relationships

This area might include people you socialize with, pets, your connections to others in your life, the quantity and quality of friends, etc.

I define close relationships as

I give away my power to

when I

because

On a scale of 1-10 rate how satisfied you are with your close relationships.
(1 = yuck, 10 = woo-hoo)

Love Life

This area might include love, marriage, divorce, romantic relationships, etc.

I define love life as

I give away my power to

when I

because

On a scale of 1-10 rate how satisfied
you are with your love life.
(1 = yuck, 10 = woo-hoo)

Personal Growth

This area might include personal awareness, self-discovery, spirituality, what you do to learn or improve yourself, etc.

I define personal growth as

I give away my power to

when I

because

On a scale of 1-10 rate how satisfied
you are with your personal growth.
(1 = yuck, 10 = woo-hoo)

Physical Surroundings

This area might include your home, office, neighborhood, possessions, clutter, etc.

I define physical surroundings as

I give away my power to

when I

because

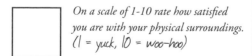

*On a scale of 1-10 rate how satisfied
you are with your physical surroundings.
(1 = yuck, 10 = woo-hoo)*

Work

This area may include your current job, one you would like to have, your career, the environment where you work, retirement, etc.

I define work as

I give away my power to

when I

because

On a scale of 1-10 rate how satisfied
you are with your work.
(1 = yuck, 10 = woo-hoo)

Money

This area may include how secure you feel financially, preparation for retirement, knowing your assets, your financial legacy, etc.

I define money as

I give away my power to

when I

because

On a scale of 1-10 rate how satisfied you are with the money in your life.
(1 = yuck, 10 = woo-hoo)

Charting Where You Are Now

Time to capture a high-level view of your life, as you are living it right now. Complete the graph below, placing a dot to represent your satisfaction with each segment of your life. Then connect the dots.

	Physical Well-being	Rejuvenation	Close Relationships	Love Life	Personal Growth	Physical Surroundings	Work	Money
10								
9								
8								
7								
6								
5								
4								
3								
2								
1								

Now notice—odds are that you do not have a straight line. This exercise is not about having a straight line or about having "high" scores across all areas of your life. This is about where you are right now. Pay attention to the peaks and the valleys. What areas call out for attention? Which ones make you smile? Are there any surprises?

Step back and think about what this graph visually says about your current reality. What is it trying to tell you?

Who are you being when you are making these choices? You might be the "good girl", the "career woman", the "cowardly lion", the "martyr", the "self-sacrificing" woman", etc.

How does it feel to give away your power?

Where are your feelings of dissatisfaction? And how do they appear in your body?

What benefits are you getting by staying stuck, unfulfilled, and dissatisfied in these areas of your life?

Now weigh the consequences of giving your power away against your desire for change. What do you notice?

In Real Life...

FROM A CLIENT

I always thought I had it all together. Sure, there were bumps in the road, days of high stress, and too many people clamoring for my attention. But isn't everyone's life like this? And besides, there are so many people who have it much worse than I do. So, why should I have anything to complain about? I mean, my life's pretty good, right?

Then I was encouraged to more closely examine the areas of my life, and discovered some rather surprising things:

> ➢ I was neglecting my health and self-care because it was more important to care for others.

> ➢ I was making my career more important than those who make my life worthwhile.

> ➢ My love life was lacking passion.

> ➢ Personal growth – Really? Who has time?

> ➢ My home environment was cluttered, I had too much stuff, and it offered no sanctuary.

Wow - what an eye-opener! So I guess that's what this empty feeling is all about. I decided I needed to make some changes.

Meditation Moment

These moments will be sprinkled throughout the book to help you fully reflect on your discoveries and desires. Meditation will help you listen to your heart so you can better discover your true voice and your deepest desires for a fulfilling life.

Plan on sitting quietly for at least ten minutes in a place where you will not be interrupted by people or technology. How you sit is not as important as finding a comfortable spot for your meditation time. You want to physically be comfortable so you can let go completely and relax into the meditation.

To begin: close your eyes and notice your breath. Feel it flowing in and out. Don't do anything, just notice. In and out. In and out. Scan your body for any feelings of tension. If you encounter any tightness, breathe into the area, offering release. Breathe in and breathe out. In and out.

Once you are fully aware of your breath and you have released any tight spots, begin to deepen your breath by extending your inhale a bit longer and your exhale a bit longer. Continue extending your inhale and exhale until you feel calm and relaxed.

———•———

Now, ask your heart to answer this question: "What do I want *right now*?"

———•———

Just sit quietly. If chatter appears in your mind, notice it and then gently dismiss it. This is normal. Come back to your breath and feel it flowing in and out. Often, slowly asking the question, in conjunction with the breath, "What do I want" (inhale), "Right now" (exhale), will help keep you focused. Let whatever arises do so without judgment. Just notice it. And with each breath let go, again and again.

———•———

When you are ready to end your meditation, do so with slow deliberation. Continue to breathe easily for several more minutes. When the time is right, slowly open your eyes. You may want to capture any insights, images, or feelings that may have arisen. Record them here or in your journal.

———•———

And, don't be discouraged if there is no revelation. Accept whatever shows up. Remember you can return to this meditation any time you want.

"It's not hard to make decisions when you know what your values are."

—Roy Disney

Your Values:
the Guideposts

In the previous section you explored the details of giving away your power. And you examined the dissatisfaction that is present in your life. You have given words and structure to your dissatisfaction, creating a greater understanding of your current reality. Keep in mind that it is the awareness that matters. If you are aware, you can consciously choose to adopt different behavior.

Choice. That's where your power comes alive. *You are in charge of your choice!* And yet knowing that you have a choice is only a part of your power. You also must recognize that you always have options, and, most importantly, that you need to select one that truly resonates with who you are becoming.

First, you need to become deeply in touch with what you *do* want. You need to be able to truly have a sense of the future. You need to be able to see it, feel it, and develop a craving for it. This is not about how you get there. (We'll come to that later on.) This is about creating an image, so fully fleshed out, so alive, that your heart sings just thinking about it.

This is all about you, free from the judgment and opinions of others. This is you leading a wildly fulfilling life. This is you, without restraint, being fully alive.

Time for a self-check. Has your inner critic joined in this conversation? Have the "yes, buts…" begun to appear? Beginning to feel a bit selfish? Feeling that you should be happy with what you already have? I mean, after all, there are so many with less than you have. Right?

ALL OF THIS IS NORMAL.

Your inner critic loves the status quo and will go to great lengths to remind you that it is really not in your best interest to disturb things. Even thinking thoughts of change, calls your inner critic forth —to protect your current state and not rock the boat. So, for now, let's agree to set these thoughts aside. Firmly tell your inner critic to be patient. There will be time to deal with it a bit later. Know that your inner critic will get lots of attention when we move into the entire chapter devoted just to this pest!

Firmly tell your inner critic to be patient.

Identifying Your Values

Your values are who you truly are, at your core. Values are how you express yourself in the world; they are evident in what you do and how you act. Values are neither right nor wrong. They just are. And, they are unique to you. Your sense of fulfillment depends upon how fully you live these personal core values, and how well your heart, head, and will are aligned.

Like runway lights on a dark, foggy night, your values guide you through the murky soup, clearly marking your path into the unknown. When you need to make a choice, ask yourself how each option honors your values. You even may discover that some choices actually step on your values! When your values are not being honored you may feel out of sorts, that your life is not in harmony or that something is missing. The secret to leading your most fulfilling life is to consciously make choices that resonate with your values.

So, let's dig in and get really specific about your unique set of values.

Clarify Your Values

Take some time to reflect and respond to these questions.

No one truly knows how long they will be on this earth. What if you learned that your time remaining will be three months or less? Knowing this, what will you do with the time you have left? Write whatever comes to mind. Dream big! Don't worry about the "how"; just write down the dreams as they come to you. Give yourself permission to let your inner voice have the spotlight.

Now that your juices are flowing, and you feel the urgency to be fully alive in your final days, let's dig a little deeper.

Think back on your childhood. When did you feel most alive? What were you doing? What was present that made you grin from the inside out?

What did you value in both of these experiences?

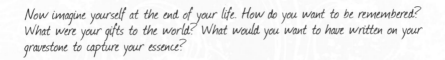

Now imagine yourself at the end of your life. How do you want to be remembered? What were your gifts to the world? What would you want to have written on your gravestone to capture your essence?

What made your life "well-lived"?

Think of someone you deeply admire. What qualities draw you to that person? Circle the top five qualities you admire.

Imagine yourself at your very best. Who are you then? What traits do you notice about yourself? Aim for capturing at least twenty!

Which of these traits are you particularly proud of having? Highlight them.

Narrowing It Down

You're almost there! Look back over your answers and list those that jumped out at you. Go with your gut. Which ones made you feel truly alive, created a really big grin on your face, or made you say, "Of course!"

Which answers are the deep-down-inside, real you? Let your heart speak freely, for it knows these truths.

The next step will help you refine your previous responses into succinct values. Perhaps you wrote, "I want to spend quality time with my family" or "I like working as part of a team." These really aren't values but give an indication of the values being honored. Remember, values are how you show up in the world, evidenced in your behavior.

So, let's continue to reduce these answers down to their essence, in a one or two word phrase. A simple way to reduce your statements is to ask why—what is the reason behind each answer.

In the first example, "I want to spend quality time with my family," what is the ultimate reason behind this statement? Perhaps it is a sense of connectedness or desiring a happy, loving family. These values would be connectedness or family.

In the second example, "I like working as part of a team," the purpose might be a sense of collaboration, or feeling part of a larger group. Here the values would be collaboration, cooperation, or relatedness.

In both cases these are my words. You may have a different way of summarizing the examples. Your values belong to you and need to be expressed in your own words.

Your values belong to you and need

Claim Your Core Values

Time to pare down your list to the five core values that truly resonate with you, that define you as you want to be in the world, that serve as the guideposts in your life.

What five values must you have in your life? Which ones speak to you on the deepest level?

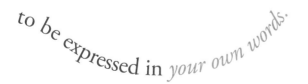

to be expressed in your own words.

It is very important to honor your values as you make choices in your life. And keep in mind that honoring your values can take many forms. Because one value is of the utmost importance to you, you may consciously choose to increase its presence in your daily life immediately. You also may choose to more fully integrate your values by taking baby steps.

No matter what you decide to do, remember that these are your values and your choices. You have the power to determine how and when you honor them.

One way you can keep these values alive in your mind is to create a values poster or collage. Use magazine pictures, words cut from newspapers, or appropriate quotes that embody your core values. I also have included inspirational quotations at the end of this workbook. Once you have created your values poster, display it where you will be able to see it at least once a day. Then take it one step further. At the end of each day, use this poster to assess how many of these values have been part of your day. Which values did you step on? Remember: honoring your values each and every day, even in bite-sized portions, will create a deliciously fulfilling life.

Honoring your values each and every day, even in bite-sized portions, will create a deliciously fulfilling life.

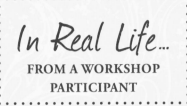

When I was asked at a recent workshop what values drive my life, I really had to pause. Well, I knew I had to have values; everyone has values. But I was hard-pressed to name them. The workshop leader put us through a series of exercises, categorizing and prioritizing. When I had completed the tasks, my response was, "Of course, that's me!" I had described myself perfectly.

Then I had to examine how often these values show up in my daily life. I came to the conclusion that their appearance was haphazard and after-the-fact. Values *driving* my life? I don't think so.

My values are important to me. So why wasn't I living them more fully? I realized I was letting circumstances and others dictate when my values were being honored. Okay, I get it. I need to take the driver's seat.

Meditation Moment

In this meditation you will reflect on what have you learned about yourself and your values. Again, plan on sitting quietly where you will be undisturbed for at least ten minutes.

———◆———

Center yourself by closing your eyes and focusing on your breath. Feel it flowing in and out. Don't *do* anything, just notice. In and out. In and out. Slowly scan your body breathing release into any areas of tension. Breathe in and breathe out. In and out.

———◆———

Once you are fully aware of your breath and you have released any tight spots, begin to deepen your breath by extending your inhale a bit longer and your exhale a bit longer. Continue extending your inhale and exhale until you feel calm and relaxed.

———•———

Now, ask yourself what your answers revealed about your values and their importance—on the deepest level. Which responses caused your heart to race, made you feel completely alive, or left you wanting more? Relish the outward glow of your true, authentic self.

———•———

At the end of your meditation, give thanks for becoming more attuned to the real you, your truest self. Record any thoughts or insights here or in your journal.

"Seek out that particular mental attribute which makes you feel most deeply and vitally alive, along with which comes the inner voice which says, 'This is the real me,' and when you have found that attitude, follow it."

—**William James**

Who DO You Want to Be?

You've spent some time determining where you give away your power and why. You've indicated how satisfied you are with the major areas of your life. And, you've identified your core values.

Now we are going to knit them together to fully envision what your most wildly fulfilling life will be like.

The time has come to add tinder to your spark!

Putting Your Core Values into Action

Look back at your five core values. For this exercise, you will expand on each by describing it more clearly and discover exactly what it means to you. Remember that values appear through your behavior, in how you present yourself in the world. And, you will brainstorm how each value might manifest itself in your life. If necessary, remind your inner critic that its chapter will appear soon.

Label each Value and then answer the following questions:
A: *What exactly does this mean to you? Be as specific as you can.*
B: *If your life had an abundance of this value, who would you be? How would others know this was your value?*

Value #1 is

A:

B:

Value #2 is

A:

B:

Value #3 is

A:

B:

Value #4 is

A:

B:

Value #5 is

What exactly does this mean to you? Be as specific as you can.

If your life had an abundance of this value, who would you be? How would others know this was your value?

Now imagine. If I waved a magic wand over you and your life became a perfect harmony of all of these values, what would change?

What gifts would be here for you?

What would your life be like if this became your reality?

What is important to you about having these values more present in your life?

I am learning that my values need to play a larger role in my life. My assignment was to list ways to honor my value of creativity. I love the feeling I get when I'm taking photographs. Time has no meaning. My stress fades away, and I experience a greater sense of aliveness. I am calm and focused. I love who I am at those moments.

So, why wasn't I seeking more of this feeling? Powerful question. I get it: I'm in control of this! I'm choosing to have more creativity in my life. It's important to who I am and it rejuvenates me. I am going to insist on having this in my weekly activities. I've even purchased a small camera, which I carry at all times. No more excuses!

Meditation Moment

In this meditation you will reflect on your life as a complete manifestation of your core values. Again, plan to sit quietly and undisturbed for at least ten minutes.

Center yourself by closing your eyes and focusing on your breath, and then slowly scan your body, using your breath to release any areas that might be straining or feeling tight. Breathe in and breathe out. In and out. Becoming more and more aware of your breath.

Now begin to deepen your breath by extending your inhale a bit longer, and your exhale a bit longer. Continue to extend your inhale and exhale until you feel calm and relaxed.

From this place of calmness, envision your life filled with opportunities to honor your core values. How does this life look to you? Notice what resonates with you. What's exciting and satisfying about this life?

Now engage all of your senses. Notice any sensations that appear in your body. What are you wearing and how does it fit? Where are you? What can you see from this place? What images or colors are here for you? What sounds are present? What vibrations do you feel? What tastes come to mind? What do you notice about the climate, the temperature, and your level of comfort?

Relish this feeling of fulfillment. This is a life of purpose, deep meaning, and great satisfaction.

At the end of your meditation, give thanks for this glimpse into the possibilities before you. Make any notations to capture this experience here or in your journal.

"We have met the enemy and he is us."

—Walt Kelly, Pogo cartoon strip

Hello, Inner Critic!

Time to give your inner critic the spotlight it craves and address the "yes, buts…," the "should's," and the "you're not good enough…" messages that tend to appear whenever you consider changing something in your life.

Usually your inner critic lurks in the background, keeping its watchful eyes on your thoughts and behaviors, vigilant for changes to the status quo. But let's be clear: your inner critic has only one job— *to protect you from yourself by intervening when you venture beyond your current reality.*

You may be saying, "Well, that doesn't make any sense. Doesn't my inner voice protect me from unsafe risks, keep me on the 'straight and narrow," and help me *know* my limits?"

Interesting. Could that be your inner critic asking those questions?

What makes you think you have limits? Or that you must follow certain rules? Why do you keep judging yourself against other people's standards or expectations?

Your inner critic is your self-sabotaging voice! It constrains you from living your most fulfilling, value-filled life. It shouts, "Danger! Danger!" to keep you in line. It allows you to live comfortably with self-limiting beliefs. *It keeps you small.*

And no you longer want to live small, do you? You want to honor your values, to make conscious choices, and to live outside of your self-imposed box. You want to reclaim your power!

So let's meet your inner critic head-on. Let's dig deeply and really define what it looks like, acts like and how it makes you feel. Let's find a way to get out of your own way so you can expand the possibilities and get on with your life in a much bigger way.

How do you know when your inner critic is actively nearby? When does it appear?

What does it look like? What metaphor might capture its essence? What name might you give it?

What are your inner critic's habits? Where does it go when it's not pestering you?

Remember this list? These are some words that your inner critic may lob at you whenever you consider moving outside of your comfort zone, playing "outside of the box" or wanting to explore the unknown or "forbidden." It's the voice that says, "If you make this choice, you most certainly will be:

REJECTED,
     laughed at,
          poor,
               WRONG,
                    all alone,
                         embarrassed,
DISAPPOINTING SOMEONE,
               found out,
                   selfish,
                         and on, and on, and on."

What is your inner critic fond of saying to you?

How does it distract you from honoring your values?

As a final exercise, you may want to draw a picture of what your inner critic looks like or find some representation of it to keep its characteristics in mind. Perhaps one word or color or even a smell captures its essence. Where might you put this image/word/color as a reminder that your inner critic is not you and that you can consciously choose to control it?

Let's face it: rocking the boat causes uncertainty and ambiguity. Your inner critic is nourished by one thing: fear. Plain and simple.

Interrupting: Hey, What Are *You* Doing Here?

So, while you are determined to move steadily onward, you know that your inner critic is lurking in the shadows. Or perhaps it has boldly stepped between you and your developing fire. Either way, it's time to decide how to deal with this pest because this time you are determined to stoke and guard your newly emerging fire! You are going to be in the driver's seat and your inner critic will be riding in the trunk on this journey.

This pest has appeared because it wants attention. It's like a fussy, demanding two-year-old. "Me! Me! Pay attention to me!" Give it attention, if only briefly, and you placate it for a while. Ignore it, and it becomes more insistent, plays on your fears and nibbles away at your strength and resolve causing you to doubt yourself.

Take heart! You do have choices for dealing with this persistent inner critic. And, over time, as you learn to deal firmly with it, it actually becomes weaker and loses much of its ability to influence your decisions.

You know you're tired of this dance you do with your inner critic. You're ready to wrest the controls away from it. Time to take a stand! So, what are your options?

You can be firm, clear and direct with it. Thank it for having served you well in the past, and sternly tell it that *you are now ready to take charge.* You are eager to move beyond the same-old, same-old and take risks. You know that you may stumble or fall and accept that this is part of the journey. You

> *You know that you may stumble or fall and accept that this is part of the journey. You are confident and primed to try new things!*

…determined to stoke and guard your newly emerging fire!

are confident and primed to try new things! Your goal is so delicious that your inner critic is not going to thwart you.

Not yet feeling ready to confront your inner critic head-on? Divert it. Give it something else to do or another place to go while you are tending your fire. You might say to yourself, "Inner critic (or the name you have given this little guy), I'm going to drop you in my desk drawer for now. I have important things to do without your interference." It is important to consciously remove it for the time being. Use your imagination.

An alternative is to recall the metaphor, word, image, etc. that you used to capture the essence of your inner critic. Now visualize your inner critic on your shoulder. Take extreme delight it forcefully flicking it away.

Be assured: when you stand up to your inner critic and confront it with your desire to create a most audacious and wildly fulfilling life, true to your core values, your inner critic will shrivel and melt just like the Wicked Witch of the West in the *Wizard of Oz*. Can't you just hear it, "I'm melting! I'm melting!!"

You are going to be in the driver's seat and your inner critic will be riding in the trunk on this journey.

What will you do, how will you be, or what will you remember to keep your inner critic at bay?

Revisiting and relishing what fulfills you in your life, envisioning your life as homage to your core values, feeling deep within your heart what you truly want in your life—all of these techniques will help you regain your power over your inner critic.

> *You must be **driven** to create the necessary changes.*

If you need to create a more enticing, can't-live-without-it vision for your future, review your responses to the core values exercises. Have you truly described your most fulfilling life? One that fully honors your core values? Have you recognized the many gifts and possibilities awaiting you? Your vision must be so compelling that you can no longer tolerate the status quo. You must be driven to create the necessary changes.

And, just a reminder: other people's expectations can throw water on your burgeoning fire, too. These options work equally as well with them.

In Real Life...

FROM A CLIENT

Sometimes I'm my worst critic. I really beat up on myself. I think things I'd never say to a family member or my best friend. I go over and over what I should have done or said. The images and words are in constant replay mode. And when I do succeed at something, I discount my actions and never really take credit.

I've finally decided this is the year of me. I want to feel better about myself. I want to let go of the past. I want to treat myself as I would my best friend. I want to believe that I am enough. The voices and images in my head have gotta go.

Meditation Moment

In this meditation you will reflect on what your life will be like as you choose to take charge over your inner critic. Dive into the possibilities of a life without self-limitation. Again, plan on sitting quietly and undisturbed for at least ten minutes.

———◆———

Center yourself by closing your eyes and focusing on your breath, then scanning your body and releasing any areas of tension. Continue to deepen your breath and welcome the sensation of complete relaxation.

———◆———

From this quiet place, envision living your life completely fulfilling your heart's desires, feeling the expansiveness created by limitless possibility. Listen to what you're heart is saying to you. Let yourself go—and dream.

———•———

Again, notice what arises within you. Where is there excitement? What is juicy here? Be aware of any sensations that appear in your body. What gifts are awaiting you?

———•———

At the end of your meditation, thank your heart for awakening you to possibilities and for the courage to make them your reality. Record any thoughts or insights here or in your journal.

"It takes courage
to grow up and
turn out to be
who you really are."

—e.e. cummings

The F- Word

F-E-A-R: the propellant that allows your inner critic to fly into action. It can show up as a gnawing feeling that causes you to doubt your capabilities, pass judgment on your physical appearance, or believe that you don't have the answers to your burning questions.

There really are two kinds of fear: healthy (keeping you away from actual harm) and unhealthy (limiting internal beliefs). One keeps you safe; one holds you back.

Yes, fear has its place, but your inner critic is *overly cautious* and lives in the realm of limiting beliefs! It's comfortable with the way things are. It feels secure in certainty, in the mundane, and within the confines of other people's expectations. And, your inner critic's timing is perfect, rearing its ugly head just at the moment you most need to be courageous, to take risks that will lead to a more fulfilling life, to spread your wings and soar toward the stars.

Unfortunately, it takes energy to wrestle with this inner critic. So you settle into a life of resignation, believing that's the way life is supposed to be. You find that you are "shoulding" all over yourself. You allow these self-limiting beliefs to stand in the way of achieving your desires. You settle.

There's a slogan used in Twelve-Step Fellowships that is equally appropriate here:

FALSE
EXPECTATIONS
APPEARING
REAL

Before you can fully appreciate this slogan, we need to examine this phrase piece by piece. And, remember, we are talking about the unhealthy kind of fear. This is not about stepping off the curb of a busy intersection without looking for on-coming traffic.

> *False* Is what you believe really true? Or is it coming from a belief that you *hold* to be true? Is it coming from your own, inner voice, the very core of you? Or is it the echo of someone else? Are you being completely honest with yourself?

> *Expectations* What obligations are you imposing on yourself? What is your perspective? Are you only predicting one possible outcome (usually a negative one)?

> *Appearing* What assumptions are you making? Are you viewing this from only one angle? Are you relying on past experience to predict this outcome?

> *Real* What facts support your viewpoint? What are you *imagining* will happen? Where is your certainty coming from?

> *Our beliefs are built from our perceptions of reality and the expectations of others.*

Synthesizing and summarizing these components boils down to one major point: fear is based on *your own perception*. It is something that you create. And often what you create is based on the *possibility* of negative things happening. Your perception of reality keeps you safe—and small.

Far too often what we believe about our capabilities and ourselves is distorted. Our beliefs are built from our perceptions of reality and the expectations of others. And keep in mind; your fears would not exist if they weren't serving you in some way.

Labeling your fears helps to *diffuse their power*

and looking *behind the fear* to what is

really going on, *will help you* begin to see

how you are *imposing limits on yourself.*

Examining Your Fears

So let's get to the heart of it and take a closer look at your fears. Labeling them helps to diffuse their power and looking behind the fear to what is really going on, will help you begin to see how you are imposing limits on yourself.

Think of some times when your inner critic put in an appearance. Perhaps you were considering a new job, wanting to expand your education, or wishing for a day just for yourself. And, predictably on cue, your inner critic begins to intone the familiar phrases: "You could never…," "Who do you think you are?" "Are you crazy?" "Aren't you selfish?" "Yes, but you promised…" "You know, you really should be…."

In the following exercises you will look at situations in your life where fear plays a part in the choices you make. As you describe your fear, be really specific. For example, instead of saying "people will think I'm too pushy," write, "If I fully participate in discussions and stand up for my ideas, people will think I am too pushy."

For each Situation, answer the following questions.
A: *What are you afraid of here? Why does your fear make perfect sense?*
What is it serving? What story are you telling yourself in order to believe this?
B: *What might you believe in order to counter this fear? (For example, the*
only way I'll know if I will fail or succeed is just to try. No one can make me
feel stupid unless I let them.)

Situation 1
Describe it here.

A:

B:

Situation 2
Describe it here.

A:

B:

Situation 3
Describe it here.

A:

B:

Time for a reminder: your answers to any of the questions in this book belong to you. There is no right or wrong way; there is only your way. Ask yourself, "Am I being honest with myself?" You may answer, "Yes!". And, if the answer is "No" ask yourself what might be going on here. Either way, you are extending your self-understanding.

Evaluating Your Potential to Change

Now summarize your three fears and rate how willing you are to move beyond each, using these rating indicators:

- ➢ 1 = Enough already - I'm done with it!
- ➢ 2 = Hmm, perhaps there's the possibility of moving past it.
- ➢ 3 = Are you kidding? This is way too scary!

FEAR #1

FEAR #2

FEAR #3

What do you notice about your willingness to move beyond your fears? Are you willing to tackle at least one of them? Or do you notice that you are not quite ready to address any of them?

Either way, recognize that making changes in your life is unsettling and will cause your fears to make themselves known. You have a choice in how you decide to deal with them. If you recognize that your fears loom large, holding you back from moving toward your dreams, they may still be serving some part of you that is unwilling to let go.

Let me help clarify with an example. Suppose you fear having your family disagree with you. How might this fear still be serving you? Is it a way of getting their attention;? Does it reinforce your belief that you lack power? Is this a method of staying connected and not feeling so alone?

Whatever your situation, take some time to explore further.

What have you learned as a result of this exercise?

Time to bring out the magic wand again. It has the power to whisk away your fears, self-judgments, and limiting self-beliefs. It gives you the power to design your reality, dissolves all rules, and wipes "should" and "yes, but" from your vocabulary. The wand allows you to hear your own true voice very clearly.

Take a moment, wave this magic wand, and send your fears scattering to the wind. Settle in and quietly listen. What would you have in your life if you knew that you could not fail, that you were safe from harm, and that joy would most definitely fill your heart?

Write your desire here. And make it something your REALLY want.

Tune in to what you are feeling right now and record what you notice.

If your fears are still hovering nearby, it could indicate that your heart's desire is not vivid enough or your longing for it is not strong enough to outweigh your fears. If this is the case, consider spending some time imagining what gifts will come with having your heart's desire. Who will you be? How will you feel? What joy will you find there? What would it be like if you began to act as if the desire was already your reality? When you have made your desire so vivid, so delicious that you are drooling with the anticipation of making it real, then proceed with the rest of this chapter.

Making a Distinction

Can you feel the difference that results from concentrating on your desire rather than on the fear? What you really want is distinctly separate from any fear that may arise. That is a very important difference!

Change is hard and requires you to assume new behaviors, practice new ways of thinking, and enter uncharted territory—all signals for your inner critic to make a grand entrance. The good news is that you have the option of making a conscious choice: move out of your comfort zone or allow your fears to keep you in your current reality.

Stating what you want or desire can be scary. Often the act of saying it out loud or writing it down translates into, "Now I have to do something about this." Say hello to the land of discomfort.

You may long for guarantees of success or a smooth ride. You may be unsure of your level of determination or your ability to remain in

> *You have the option of making a conscious choice: move out of your comfort zone or allow your fears to keep you in your current reality.*

action. You may want to have someone just *tell* you how to be. The journey may drain you, especially when your actions require a new state of being in the world.

This is where your support network or a life coach can help you by providing unconditional encouragement and new perspectives, all the while offering you sanctuary and spaciousness to explore.

Choosing Your Perspective

So, who do *you* want to be in charge of your life: you or your inner critic? What is your choice: living life small or living fully engaged? Aren't you tired of this inner critic having the upper hand?

Remember: fear comes from *your perception* that you cannot act or will act incorrectly. You have chosen this negative perception, so why not *choose to replace it* with a more positive perception? Even though you are feeling really scared, tell yourself that you are going to do it anyway, no matter what happens. In many cases you will find that your perceived fears didn't have any foundation or they were completely exaggerated.

Make a commitment to yourself to honor your dream and live large. And, to give your dream even greater power, share it with a trusted friend. Your inner critic will still put up a fight; it's really persistent. So, when your fears pop up, ask yourself how you might honor your commitment, even in a very small way. Each time you chose the path to your heart's desire, your inner critic grows weaker. Baby steps or giant leaps, you are in motion!

What gifts await you? Each time you change your perception and push onward anyway, you conquer a bit of your fear. You feel pride in accomplishing something you initially thought you could not do. You knock through one more barrier on your path to the powerful, fully alive you! And know that this gets easier over time. Courage is like a muscle—it gets stronger with use.

I invite you to make a conscious choice to regain your power, to recognize that you really have no limits, that you have a right to step into your most unique, audacious self! You deserve to live your most delicious life!

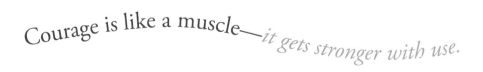

Courage is like a muscle—it gets stronger with use.

"Girls can do anything." Yeah, right. I never fully believed this. Society put up too many roadblocks. Other people said I couldn't and I believed them; and frankly, I was afraid to rock the boat.

And then I had a daughter. Watching her grow I realized how much I wanted for her. I didn't want her to be afraid to try things and take risks like me. I wanted everything possible for her. I was really putting this into action, watching her blossom and take risks, and then it hit me: "Why can't I do the same thing?" Okay, so I'm not ready to take a giant step, but I do know that I am ready to make my fears and hesitation a lot less intrusive.

Meditation Moment

In this meditation you will take time to visualize that you are fearless and can do anything your heart calls you to do. Reflect on the possibilities that open up to you. Recognize the power within yourself. Again, plan on sitting quietly and undisturbed for at least ten minutes. In this case, more time is better!

———✦———

Center yourself, by closing your eyes and focusing on your breath, then scanning your body, breathing release into any areas of tension. Begin to deepen your breath and ease into the sensation of relaxation.

———✦———

From this peaceful place, envision yourself as a superpower. You have no fear because normal human beings cannot harm you, either physically or by words. You may falter or fail in your attempts, but you *cannot be harmed*. Revel in the expansiveness of this perspective.

———•———

Again, notice what arises within you. What does your heart tell you is possible? What feelings are here? Where does your power show up in your body? What do you notice about your energy level? What is its source? Listen to your heart. What is it telling you? What feelings capture your essence?

———•———

What possibilities are now available to you?

———•———

At the end of your meditation, give thanks to your superpower for showing you how invincible you are. And know that you can call on this superpower again. Capture your experience here or in your journal.

Quick Re-cap

Let's do a quick check-in. Here is what you have accomplished so far. You have:

> ➤ identified where you give away your power, across the many segments of your life
> ➤ clarified your core values
> ➤ envisioned living your life with an abundance of these core values
> ➤ met your inner critic, and
> ➤ examined your fears and their effect on your choices.

Stop! Don't proceed further until you take a moment to recognize the work you have done. The inner soul-searching has not been easy. Applaud your determination. Celebrate your progress. Honor your commitment to yourself.

>< >< >< >< >< >< >< >< >< >< >< >< >< ><

You are now ready to rekindle your inner fire, to become who you were meant to be!

So, let's revisit the fire metaphor. You are reading this book, becoming more aware that you have a faintly glowing ember of power. It's time to tend to this ember and begin to create your blazing fire. The world is waiting for you and your unique gifts!

The world is waiting for you and your unique gifts!

First, you will need to clear your inner space of debris, broken dreams, old beliefs and others' expectations. Whose voice, other than your own, do you still hear? Any person, idea, or belief that will not, or cannot support you as you build your fire must be set aside or turned away. In your mind, visualize this clearing, free of items that will not feed your fire. Embrace this sacred space as the gateway to the most authentic you.

Next you will need to gather your kindling. Good news! You have already begun this step. You have identified your core values and how you might manifest them in the world. Purposefully gather these values and carefully create a small teepee-like structure that will encase and protect your tiny ember of power.

Take a moment and feel the ember pulsing in your heart. The time has come. You know you want more! Your journey is calling. When the "how will I…" thoughts start to appear, gently set them aside, knowing that this is not your concern right now.

This is all about embracing your ember and becoming willing to let it steadily grow into a blaze of light.

With loving care, guide this ember into your structure of core values. Take a moment and reflect on how your values—your core essence—surround and protect this ember, which, when ignited, will light your way to what you truly want in your life. It will guide you to who you are becoming.

Now notice. Slowly, deliberately, your ember begins to grow stronger. Tiny flames begin to appear. However, as with any fire, if left untended it can diminish and in time it may die out. In your heart, you know that is not what you want.

As with a fire, kindling and a spark are insufficient for a long-lasting, continuously blazing fire. You need more than your values to support your inner fire. These values merely provide a structure and a foundation for everything that will be added to the fire.

Time to add smaller branches to stoke the emerging flame. Look around you. Recall the dreams and possibilities you envisioned earlier. Look back on ways you might manifest your core values, leading you to your life purpose. Conjure what you truly want in your life and how you will feel when they become your reality. And, rest assured, they will become your reality!

...as with any fire, if left untended it can diminish and in time it may die out.

While putting words to our dreams breathes life into them; most often that is not enough. Having a support network and unconditional cheerleaders are also necessary, as are personal affirmations and a recognition that you are going to stumble, and fall and rise again, wiser for the experience.

Turning to the wisdom of the Elders in your circle of influence may offer you insights and the courage to continue. Your flame is a blend of the elements necessary to maintain its glow. And strength comes from the confluence of you and your support mechanisms.

Now, mindfully stack each of these small branches onto your values-based structure. And observe.

Each branch slowly warms, becomes part of the greater whole, and then suddenly bursts into flame, adding fuel and power to your emerging fire.

Take a moment to reflect. Your ember is encased in a framework built on solid, core values. The resulting flame is being nourished by your dreams, your desire to make a difference in the world, and by those who unconditionally support you. You are very aware of the increasing, flickering light, which more and more frequently reveals the path ahead of you.

It's important to note that progressing from ember to spark to flame is only a part of what is necessary. How you build your fire—the rate at which you add more fuel, how you stack it, and how you deal with the challenges of keeping the fire blazing—all have a direct bearing on the intensity and duration of your fire and the amount of heat and light it will provide.

You've come so far. You really want this. You are very determined to keep this fire blazing! So let's get a move on!

In your heart, you know that is not what you want.

"Asking for help does not mean we are weak or incompetent. It usually indicates an advanced level of honesty and intelligence."

—Anne Wilson Schaef

Fanning Your Fire

Defining Your Support System

All long-lasting fires need an infusion of oxygen as well as fuel. Think of your oxygen as your personal network—perhaps a life coach, affirmations, visual reminders, and your connection to your Higher Power. This is your support system—the people and things that keep you going when the path is fogged in or when you've stumbled and it's hard to get back up. They cheer you on, relentlessly and unconditionally. And, because you share your goals and dreams with them, they can hold you accountable. They can help you keep your eyes on the prize!

Time to get really clear about what constitutes your oxygen supply.

Your personal support network adds light to your journey's path and provides warmth to your heart and soul when the expectations of others threaten to freeze-dry your dreams. Those in your support system can walk with you when you grow weary, remind you that you're tougher and more courageous than you realize, and offer their wisdom and experience. They can join the battle against your fears, call you on the stories you tell yourself, and help you celebrate the "aha" moments. They can provide a safe haven, a different perspective and inspiration when you're running low.

Your only requirement is to ask them for help, which deep down, you know they will gladly provide. You don't have to create this change on your own!

It's time to clearly define your support system and make it concrete. Define who's going to be with your on this journey.

Who are the people who believe in you, no matter what? How do they show their support for you?

Who might you approach to add to your support network? What will they contribute to the mix?

Sustaining Yourself with Affirmations

In addition to your support network, you can personally bolster your determination through affirmations. A *positive* affirmation is a self-nurturing declaration, either expressed verbally or via visual representation, used to replace negative thoughts or beliefs. Note that it can be perceived. It is not a thought, which too often can be discounted by your inner critic. Affirmations keep you focused on your goal, help you continually visualize your new behavior, belief, and mental attitude, and cause you to reappraise your old beliefs to create change in your life. They keep your desire alive. They change your thoughts about a situation. They get results.

Affirmations can be demonstrated in one of these ways:

➢ **a statement of the progress you have made so far:**
- I have lost ten pounds and I'm ready to lose more!
- I am eagerly learning the skills for my next job.

➢ **a way of expressing a belief you have:**
- I will become an exceptionally caring RN.
- I can do anything I set my mind to.

➢ **an acknowledgement of who you are, at your inner core:**
- I have the power to change people's lives.
- I can survive anything.

Your affirmations are unique to you and must have an emotional impact on you. They are written in the present tense, beginning "I am…," as if you already have that quality or belief and must reflect a positive state. Remember, this is what you are striving to attain.

Now it's your turn. Review the areas of your life where you give away your power. Then choose one area, and think of a positive statement that expresses what you do want or how this area might be improved.

> *Your affirmations are unique to you and must have an emotional impact on you.*

As an example, assume that within the Friends and Family Relationships area, you let others determine how you feel by taking on their mood or perspective. You recognize that you want to own and feel your own emotions. Your affirmation might look like this:

I give myself permission to feel what I feel.
Or you might consider: **My emotions are valid and belong to me.**

The important thing is to have an emotional connection to the affirmation. You are your own best cheerleader! Only you know *exactly* what you want.

What affirmations might you give yourself to keep heading toward your goals and your new state of being?

The next step is to determine how you will use your affirmations. Remember, for affirmations to be effective, they need to be expressed verbally or via visual representation—or both! And, they need to be read, said aloud, or seen several times throughout the day.

Possible ways to keep your affirmations foremost in your mind:

> ➤ Display Post-it® notes in strategic places. (bathroom mirror, dashboard, refrigerator, etc.)

> ➤ Repeat an affirmation while looking into your mirror, and say it with gusto.

> ➤ Create an image that captures the essence of the affirmation and place it where you will see it often. And make it vivid!

> ➤ Fashion a vision board filled with pictures that capture your core values, display inspiring and encouraging words, or that celebrate who you are becoming as you reclaim your power.

> ➤ Send yourself a voicemail with your affirmation in it. Remember to save it for future listening.

> ➤ Give a friend some self-addressed and stamped cards containing an affirmation to be sent to you periodically.

> ➤ Identify your theme song, one that captures who you are becoming. Listen to it on the device of your choice or sing it in the shower every day.

> ➤ Establish a morning or evening ritual that reinforces your emerging power.

Use your creativity. Use whatever works to keep you motivated. Remember, this is the oxygen you will use to keep your fire stoked!

Record how you will keep your affirmations constantly in the forefront of your busy life.

In Real Life...

FROM A CLIENT

I owe my college degree to those who have supported me along the way. I couldn't have done it alone.

You know, making changes in my life hasn't always gone as I had expected. There were plenty of times that I almost threw in the towel. Going to college was costing too much time and money. And yet my friends were always there for me. They saw things in me that I never knew I had. They kicked my in the butt when I needed it— and boy, did I need it sometimes—and they offered a shoulder to cry on. They toasted me when I took baby steps and they never once doubted my success.

I am so thankful that they were there when I asked them to help me.

Meditation Moment

In this meditation you will spend time visualizing your support network surrounding you, bestowing strength and encouragement. Lean into their message that you are fearless and deeply loved. Truly feel their presence reminding you that you can do anything that resonates with your heart. Reflect on the possibilities that open up to you. Recognize the power within yourself.

Again, plan on sitting quietly and undisturbed for at least ten minutes, longer if possible.

———◆———

Center yourself, slowing down your breath, and consciously releasing any areas of tension. Begin to relax.

———◆———

When you are fully relaxed, picture yourself sitting before your growing fire. Feel your strong desire to create a much larger fire, a blaze. You want your fire to light up the sky. You want this fire to be awe-inspiring and powerful. You want it to have intense heat and a vital presence.

———•—•———

Now, call upon someone who provides supports for you. Feel them heed your call, without hesitation, and watch as they breathe gently onto your fire. Feel their arms wrapping around you, adding their strength to yours. And notice. What shift happens? How does your heart respond?

———•—•———

Repeat this several times, calling on others to support you. And, each time, just notice. What has happened to your fire? To your strength? To your determination?

———•—•———

Finally, repeat your own affirmations and feel their truth.

———•—•———

At the end of your meditation, breathe in who you are becoming and quietly give thanks to those who unconditionally support you. Record any thoughts or insights here or in your journal.

"You have to decide what your highest priorities are and have the courage—pleasantly, smilingly, non-apologetically—to say 'no' to other things. And the way you do that is by having a bigger 'yes' burning inside."

—Stephen Covey

Putting It All Together

The time has come. You've dreamed and envisioned what life can be like by reclaiming your power. You've discovered things about yourself, including your core values and how to handle your inner critic who delights in throwing the F-word your way. You know exactly how to ask for help and how you can affirm who you are becoming. You know that you have a choice, *and you know for certain that there is no going back to the old you.*

It's now time to step into action, move beyond the theory and create your new reality. So, take a deep breath and say, "Yes!" to becoming who you were meant to be. Acknowledge that you are ready to take a stand for what you want in your life. So let's do something about it!

Clearing Your Inner Space

To begin, ensure that you have cleared away any past debris, broken dreams, old beliefs and others' expectations. Still sound daunting? I challenge you to act "as if."

How would you proceed "as if" you could not fail? "As if" you knew exactly what you were doing? "As if" you had all of the courage you needed? "As if" your inner critic were on permanent holiday?

Check in: are there any "yes, buts" coming to the surface? Any niggling voices telling you that if you proceed, you are going to be: rejected, laughed at, poor, wrong, all alone, embarrassed, disappointing someone, found out, or selfish?

If any of these reactions appear, take it as a good sign! They indicate that you are rocking the status quo, and know that *they are of your own making*. Since you create these beliefs, you also can choose to move beyond them. So, take a few moments and breathe in love for yourself, for who you want to become. Then breathe out all of the things that no longer serve you, which no longer provide you with a sense of joy and fulfillment.

Breathe in, "I have the power to manage my life." Breathe out, "I will no longer live just to please others." Breathe in, "I am becoming who I am at my core." Breathe out, "I release all of my self-limitations." Breathe in, "I am creating a most audacious and wildly fulfilling life." Breathe out, "I will no longer neglect myself and my needs."

You are making room for something new, something yet to be discovered.

Visualize your cleared space, free from self-limiting beliefs and others' expectations. You are making room for something new, something yet to be discovered. Embrace your sacred space, your gateway to the most authentic you.

Time to live large. *Your life is calling.*

Consciously Choosing Which Fire to Build

The time has come to consciously choose where you will begin to reclaim your power. In the previous chapters we have been using an image of a single fire growing ever larger as a metaphor for your power. In reality, there are many smaller fires—indicators of your power—that represent the many segments of your life. Remember: the intensity of your fire in one area of your life reflects the intensity of your fire in all areas of your life. Augmenting your fire—ramping up your power—in one area directly impacts the magnitude of your aggregate inner fire.

In the following exercises you will start with one area so you do not become overwhelmed with too much change in your life. Review your earlier responses that describe your current reality, and then select a specific area that resonates with you, an area where you want to reclaim your power—*now*.

I have chosen to work on this area of my life:

Which I define as:

Why is it important to you to begin here?

Now consider: how will reclaiming your power in this area make a difference in your life?

What excites you about this?

What scares you about this?

Stoking Your Fire

Review your core values, the essential and intrinsic beliefs that define who you are in the world. These are your unique markers, guiding you along the decision-making points in your life, leading you to fulfillment and providing a greater sense of purpose as you honor them.

How does reclaiming your power in this area honor your core values?

What possibilities are now open to you?

What gifts will you be bringing into the world as you add power and purpose in this area of your life?

Locking in Your Learning

Stand in a way that embodies your growing power. Inhale a long, slow, deep breath. Now envision your exhale adding fuel to your fire. Feel it building within you. With each breath it grows stronger. Notice what is happening. What physical sensations appear? Notice your heart, what is happening there? Where are your eyes focused; what can you see and how well can you see it from here? Check in with your breathing; what's happening here? Scan your body for any other sensations. What else do you notice? Take your time and feel.

Now *amplify your power*. Visualize an unending source of power, enough to produce a light so brilliant that it can be seen from the furthest reaches of outer space. Feel this power coursing through every part of your body, sending electricity into the ether. Become aware of the effect this surge has on you. What has shifted? What physical changes have occurred?

What is possible from here?

And, from this position of power, certainty, and desire, what do you now have to say to your inner critic?

Keeping Your Fire Burning Brightly

Reality check: most people can't do this entirely on their own. You need to get really specific about the people and things that will help you keep going. It's time to identify your cheerleaders.

Name five people who will be there for you, relentlessly urging you on as you reclaim your power in this area. And describe how they will do this for you.

....

❶

....

❷

....

❸

....

❹

....

❺

....

Sharing a dream creates a sense of challenge and reinforces its importance. It makes the dream real.

Your next action is to tell these people your dream of a more fulfilling, powerful, and purposeful life, and to explain why it's important to you. This will give vibrancy to your dream and will diminish the chances that you will begin to waver, make excuses, or change your mind and give up. Sharing a dream creates a sense of challenge and reinforces its importance. *It makes the dream real.*

Creating change requires courage. Make a pledge to yourself that you will continue onward, even when you are scared or uncomfortable, and especially when your inner critic begins to use a megaphone to get your attention. Remember: use your support network! They are there for you. They want you to succeed. They will help you up when you stumble or fall, and they will support you when you are tired, feeling lost, or struggling with roadblocks. Use them!

Now, how will you support and take care of yourself? We all know that the busyness of life has a way of interrupting momentum and focus. You will need to keep the dream alive and in the forefront of your mind. Periodically you will need to restore your spirit and energize. Remember: this is not about success or failure; this is about trying to change and moving toward the authentic you. Each time you rise, you become stronger. This is about your journey and not your destination.

If you haven't done so previously, write one or two affirmations to support you along the way. Keep in mind that they must have an emotional impact on you and naturally reflect a positive statement.

Specifically, how will you keep these messages alive for yourself? How can you make them fun?

You also need to prepare for those down days. The ones where you'd rather hide in the closet than face the world. So, let's think ahead.

What loving words will you say to yourself when you encounter a roadblock or stumble or fall?

And how are you going to care for yourself?
(A daily nurturing activity would be delicious, but at the very least, schedule something once a week.)

What promise can you make to yourself to replenish your spirit before it is depleted?

In Real Life...

FROM A CLIENT

Before—that's what I call my previous lack of power—I was the one my parents, my kids, and my brother and his kids turned to when they needed something. Things like running errands or babysitting. And, of course, I never turned any of them down. Oh, and did I mention that I work full-time and am a single mom? I used to fall into bed completely exhausted and feeling depleted. And then I'd wake the next day and start the merry-go-round again.

One day I decided something had to give because no one was taking care of me! I spent some time working on myself and realized that I had power over how I spent my time. I reestablished my priorities and learned to say no, nicely, of course, and also firmly. Best of all, I made a commitment to take time for myself every day. Sometimes it's only 30 minutes to read. Other times it's an evening with friends. Often it's a nice, long, hot bath without my little helpers. And I don't feel guilty in the least! I have learned that taking care of me helps me to be more present with my kids. And they're the most important people in my life.

Self-care is my way of saying. "I'm important, too!"

Saying YES to Your Fire

The time for commitment has arrived. You have cleared space for who you will be in the world as you reclaim your power, given your inner critic a piece of your mind, and identified ways to support yourself on this journey.

Let's clarify what you truly are welcoming into your life by examining what you are saying YES and NO to as you move forward.

Think of saying NO as a means to creating room for what you want more of in your life. Saying NO allows you to move beyond the self-limiting beliefs, behaviors, and feelings that no longer serve who you are becoming. You are ready to move on. You've said it in so many ways throughout this book. You want so much more. Let's make room by saying NO and letting these things go.

What old beliefs, behaviors and feelings are you saying NO to?

❶ ....

❷ ....

❸ ....

❹ ....

❺ ....

Now notice. Do you need to mourn the release of these old ways of being? If so, consider some possible ways to move beyond them:

➤ List these five items on a piece of paper, and then burn it.

➤ Create a personal release ceremony.

➤ Write a letter to the old you, explaining why you are moving on.

➤ Draw a tombstone and list the items and their dates of existence.

And, now the juicy part: welcoming in the things you are saying YES to in your life! You know that these will bring you greater fulfillment and purpose. You know that they honor your values. Welcome your most audacious and passion-filled life.

What are you joyously, loudly, and emphatically saying YES to?

❶ ....

❷ ....

❸ ....

❹ ....

❺ ....

> Keep in mind that saying NO will come more and more easily as you become more intently focused on your bigger YES, aligning your choices with what matters most in your life.

Springing into Action

Put your future in good hands—your own. —Author Unknown

You know where you are headed, the longing is there, the possibilities are emerging, your support is defined, and you've told your inner critic to take a nice, long vacation in a remote corner of the world. You no longer want to live small. You are ready to take a stand for what you want in your life. You want to honor your values, to make conscious choices, and to live beyond self-limiting beliefs. You have discovered your power!

Believing and wanting is not enough though. You need action to create a life of fulfillment, purpose, and passion. You are so ready to step into your desire, to really own it, and to focus energy on creating it. Now is the time to take that first step. You may want to begin with small steps and gradually build to a full gallop, or you may want to take a giant leap right now. Either way, you need to get moving and stay in motion.

What is one action you can take now to get yourself in motion? And, what support will you need to get going?

What would it take to amplify that action ten-fold? 100-fold?

Now add strength to your desire to move toward your dreams: have someone hold you accountable for completing an action. There are three components necessary for accountability:

> ➤ Share the action you will take with someone you trust.

> ➤ Set a deadline for completion of the task.

> ➤ Decide how you will inform the one holding you accountable that you have completed what you promised.

And, sometimes you won't follow through; that's reality. There is also a lesson to be learned from this. Promise yourself that you will take time to examine the underlying reason why you did not meet your deadline. There may be many reasons, some unavoidable and some that masquerade as reasons but are actually your inner critic at work. Be honest with yourself and determine what *truly* was holding you back from your commitment. Then share that reason with someone in your trusted support network. If necessary, recall why you are making this journey, what values you are honoring, and then begin on the action again. Remember: your support network is there to help you when you stumble or fall. They will cheer you on unconditionally.

How will you acknowledge yourself once you complete this first step?

Deepening Your Learning: Wash. Rinse. Repeat.

You are on your way! You are one step closer to the life you have imagined, guided by your heart and your values. There will be many more steps along your path. It is of no concern how quickly or slowly you move forward. It is of great importance that you *continue to move forward*. There may be diversions, setbacks, or delays, but you must continue to keep moving on your path. When in doubt, rekindle the longing that propelled you on this journey.

Over time you will want to consciously choose to reclaim your power in other areas in your life. Use these same principles over and over. One of the greatest gifts of your journey is that by gaining power in one area, you will more quickly regain your power in another area. Now that's a gift worth receiving!

Basking in the Glow

Again, this is about your journey, not the destination. You have a limited vantage point right now. As you grow, the destination will change and grow as well. It is the process that causes you to develop in ways you never would have thought possible. Each action or risk you take and each time you try you bolster your courage, reinforce your resolve, and instill a greater sense of purpose in your life. And your dreams will respond in kind, growing right along with you.

You are now taking action. Step by step you are progressing toward your destination. Time to reflect for a few moments.

What has kept you going? When did you think you just couldn't continue?

What thoughts were present in each of these situations?

Which action is predominant now: moving forward or hesitating? Why?

If you are struggling to continue on your path, what can you do to bolster your courage?

Regardless of what your thinking is right now, it is time to celebrate that you have been trying, along with your successes *and* failures. Remember: *your power comes from the journey* and not the destination. Each failure offers you an opportunity to step back, learn, and then try an alternative. The more you try, the stronger you become and the less likely you are to consciously or unconsciously give away your power. Now that's worth celebrating, don't you think?

Describe how you will celebrate your journey. And, be specific: when and where will you celebrate? Your goal is to make it sooner rather than later.

FROM A CLIENT

My life was really monotonous and stifling. I'd start projects and then just leave them unfinished. I didn't have much energy. I kept hearing my spouse say, "You *should* do this. You *can't* do that. Where are *you* going?" I was getting really tired of feeling controlled by him. And I noticed that I had become an expert at negative self-talk.

One day I realized that I didn't want to live the rest of my life like this. I wanted to eliminate the negativity around me. I wanted *me* back!

So, I worked with someone who truly believed in me and helped me stay motivated. Over time I found my voice. And I came to recognize the power of words, the impact they have on my approach to life, and the expectations I have for myself.

I will no longer be squelched, put down or governed by "shoulds". I have found my own power, my self-confidence, and vitality. And it's about time!

Meditation Moment

In this final meditation you will bask in the glow of who you are becoming. Again, plan on sitting quietly and undisturbed for a minimum of ten minutes.

Center yourself and focus on your breath. Feel it softly and slowly flowing in and out. Release into any areas of tension and welcome the sensation of calm.

———•·•———

From this quiet space, envision the steady love from your support network and feel the expansive possibilities in every breath you take. Who are you becoming? Allow the fire of your power to course through your veins. What other sensations do you perceive? What is juicy in this moment?

———•·•———

Now, imagine the power of your spirit and all those who believe in you, softly embracing you, gently bolstering your courage and determination. Bask in the glow of this unconditional love. What sensations arise here?

———•———

At the end of your meditation, give thanks for the power that is growing within you. Smile at the possibilities now available to you. Again, record what you experienced in this meditation here or in your journal.

"The privilege of a life-
time is to become who
you truly are."

—Carl Gustav Jung

Where Do You Go from Here?

You are well on your way to your most audacious and wildly fulfilling life! You have consciously chosen to fuel your spark and revitalize your ember of personal power, evoking abundant possibilities. You have identified what you truly want and why it is of utmost importance to your sense of fulfillment. You are grounded by your core values and recognize how they add meaning and purpose to your life. And you are learning how to handle your inner critic and the accompanying F-word.

You have taken the first of many steps on your journey to becoming who you were meant to be and you have celebrated where you are now. Bravo!

The time has now come to send you on your way. You have the tools to manifest your heart's desires. Your compass is set. You are ready.

I celebrate your courage in taking the first of many steps. I believe that your tenacity will carry you through any challenges you may face. And I know, without any doubt, that your gifts will change the world.

Go forth and live large!

Additional Support
for Your Journey

Too often we are led to believe that we can go it alone. Or we may feel that our sources of support are not always there for us. Either way, it is important to have a strong foundation to sustain us as we are making permanent changes in our lives. We need someone to champion our vision of the person we are becoming. We need someone to walk along as we head powerfully into our futures, encouraging us to share our gifts with the world.

I have found that using a life coach has been vital to my life's journey. Working with my coach helped me go confidently toward my future: a significantly ramped up version of what I had been doing informally throughout most of my life. I truly believe in the power of life coaching, both on a personal level, and as a professional certified life coach myself.

Working with a life coach will help you build lifelong skills, increase your confidence, and find a richer, more balanced and purposeful life.

As a professional certified life coach, I offer encouragement, unconditional openness and honesty, and a safe space to grow. I ask the hard questions that sometimes may make you uncomfortable, so that you can dig down and face your fears and discover your inner truth. I will hold you accountable and kick you in the butt as needed, with your permission of course. I will hold a greater vision for you than you have for yourself, calling you forth when you impose self-limitations. Opportunities expand. Challenges are overcome. Dreams become reality.

Deciding to use a life coach indicates that you recognize the value of focused, individualized support because you have important changes to make so that your dreams can take flight. You know that all successful people rely on a coach or mentor to motivate them to soar even higher. And you want that, too.

Has this book whetted your appetite for more? Are you ready to reach higher than you ever dreamed possible? Are you ready to discover the delicious opportunities just beyond your view?

If you answered an unrestrained "Yes!" and are ready to live the most magnificently delicious and joyful life of your dreams, let's explore the possibilities.

Opportunities expand. Challenges are overcome. Dreams become reality. Let's explore the possibilities.

Inspirational Quotes

I absolutely adore inspirational quotes and I'm always on the lookout for more to add to my collection. What fascinates me is how some authors so succinctly create just the right words that capture my dreams, my view of life, my joys and emotions. I have included some of my favorites that address the concepts in this book. May they speak to you, as well.

"Our doubts are traitors and make us lose the good we oft might win by fearing to attempt."

—SHAKESPEARE

"Experience is simply the name we give our mistakes."
Oscar Wilde

"Go confidently in the direction of your dreams. Live the life

"We never know how high we are
Till we are called to rise;
And then, if we are true to plan,
Our statures touch the skies."

—Emily Dickinson

"You get in life what you have the courage to ask for."

—Oprah

"Let me listen to me and not to them."

—GERTRUDE STEIN

"The only limit to our realization of tomorrow will be our doubts of today."

Franklin D. Roosevelt

"You miss 100 percent of the shots you never take."

—Wayne Gretzky

"Success comes in cans, not can'ts."

—Author Unknown

"...you've imagined." Henry David Thoreau

"Whatever you can do or dream you can, begin it. Boldness has genius, power, and magic in it."

—GOETHE

"Risk! Risk anything! Care no more for the opinions of others, for those voices. Do the hardest thing on earth for you. Act for yourself. Face the truth."
Katherine Mansfield

Explore Further

These are some of the resources I have found especially useful as I travel my life's journey. Enjoy!

Books

ON SELF-CARE

A Woman's Book of Confidence, Meditations for Strength and Inspiration. Sue Patton Thoele. ISBN 978-1-56731-301-7.

Five Good Minutes, 100 morning practices to help you stay calm & focused all day long. Jeffrey Brantley and Wendy Millstone. ISBN 1-57224-414-3.

The Life Organizer—a Woman's Guide to a Mindful Year. Jennifer Louden. ISBN 978-57731-554-4.

The Woman's Comfort Book. Jennifer Louden. ISBN 0-06-077667-6.

The Woman's Retreat Book. A Guide to Restoring, Rediscovering, and Reawakening Your True Self—in a Moment, an Hour, a Day, or a Weekend. Jennifer Louden. ISBN 0-06-251466-0.

ON HAPPINESS

Attitudes of Gratitude. How to Give and Receive Joy Every Day of Your Life.
M. J. Ryan. ISBN 978-1-56731-372-7.

The Awe-manac—a Daily Dose of Wonder. Jill Badonsky.
ISBN 978-0-7624-3125-0.

Bring on the Joy: How to Unleash the Power of Joy in Your Life, Jen Yost.
ISBN 978-0-98928585-1-6.

The Happiness Project—or why I spent a year trying to sing in the morning,
clean my closets, fight right, read Aristotle, and generally have more fun.
ISBN 978-0-06-158326-1.

The Joy Diet, 10 Daily Practices for a Happier Life. Martha Beck.
ISBN 0-609-60990-4.

What I Wish for You, simple wisdom for a happy life. Patti Digh.
ISBN 978-0-7627-7062-5.

ON FINDING YOUR TRUE SELF

A Weekend to Change Your Life. Finding Your Authentic Self after a Lifetime
of Being All Things to All People. Joan Anderson. ISBN 978-0-7679-2055-1.

The Bigger Game, Why Playing a Bigger Game Designs Who You Want
to Become. Laura Whitworth, Rick Tamlyn and Caroline MacNeill Hall.
ISBN 978-1-4327-2416-0.

Callings. Finding and Following an Authentic Life. Gregg Levoy.
ISBN 0-609-80370-0.

Finding Your Own North Star, Claiming the Life You Were Meant to Live.
Martha Beck. ISBN 0-8129-3217-X.

Infinite Possibilities, the Art of Living Your Dreams. Mike Dooley. ISBN 978-1-58270-232-2.

I Will Not Die an Unlived Life, Reclaiming Purpose and Passion. Dawna Markova. ISBN 1-57321-101-6.

Life Is a Verb. Patti Digh. ISBN 978-1-59921-295-1.

The Not So Big Life. Sarah Susanka. ISBN 978-0-8129-7600-7.

Repacking Your Bags, Lighten Your Load for the Rest of Your Life, Richard J. Leider and David A. Shapiro. ISBN 1-881052-87-7.

Your Heart's Desire. Instructions for Creating the Life You Really Want. Sonia Choquette. ISBN 0-609-80011-6.

ON MINDFULNESS

101 Exercises for the Soul, Simple Practices for a Healthy Body, Mind & Spirit. Dr. Bernie S. Siegel. ISBN 978-1-57731-852-1.

Inner Peace for Busy People. 52 Simple Strategies for Transforming Your Life. Joan Borysenko. ISBN 1-4019-0214-6.

Living in Process. Basic Truths for Living the Path of the Soul. Anne Wilson Schaef. ISBN 0-3454-39407-0.

Now! The Art of Being Truly Present. Jean Smith. ISBN 0-86171-480-6.

The Quiet Voice of the Soul. How to Find Meaning in Ordinary Life. Tian Dayton. ISBN 1558743391.

Stopping. How to Be Still When You Have to Keep Going. David Kunditz. ISBN 1573241091.

ON SELF-HELP

Four Word Self Help, Simple Wisdom for Complex Lives. Patti Digh. ISBN 978-1-59921-980-6.

Glad No Matter What. Sark. ISBN 978-1-57731-935-1.

How to Say No…and Live to Tell about It, A Woman's Guide to Guilt-Free Decisions. Mary M. Byers. ISBN 0-7369-1687-3.

Nature and the Human Soul. Cultivating Wholeness and Community in a Fragmented World. Bill Plotkin. ISBN 1577315510.

Soulcraft. Crossing into the Mysteries of Nature and Psyche. Bill Plotkin. ISBN 1577314220.

POETRY

Billy Collins

David Whyte

Mary Oliver

Rumi

Acknowledgements

Throughout this book I have touted the benefits of a defined personal support network. Mine has sustained me, cheered me, sent my inner critic packing and helped me celebrate the baby steps and major leaps I've taken to create this book. They continually kept their faith in me and helped to nurture my germ of an idea until it has become a reality.

I ♥ you all:

The League of Heroes who continue to provide love and support.

SYM who has continuously encouraged me to soar ever higher.

The steadfast and insightful ladies who make up the European contingent.

My little brother, Kyle Stueber, who eagerly offered his publishing expertise.

Misty Wilt who always amazes me with her wildly creative designs, uplifts my spirits, and graciously shares her abundant energy.

Laura Maney who connected the dots and led me to my amazing editor.

Betty Bechtel who gently showed me that I still have a thing or two to learn about grammar, and that there are numerous ways to say "status quo".

Christy Long who opened doors, encouraged me and offered suggestions.

Mairéad Martin, Gretchen Pritts, Wilma Wijnhoven, Sue Saker, Emma Israelsson, Stephanie Yost Mentzell; all dear friends who eagerly offered to read early drafts, kept the "atta girl's" coming, and who raised a glass or two in my honor.

My courageous clients who have taught me so much as we have journeyed together.

Authors Jen Yost and Cathy Jennings who graciously shared their wisdom, resources and hindsight.

Collen Dewhurst, role model extraordinaire.

Mom, who believed in me always. I miss you!

About the Author

© heidi lynne photography

Robin Anderson, a post-WWII baby, was steeped in the traditions of a *woman's place is in the home.* In high school she learned that she could *make things happen,* but her early college years clouded that discovery. Then the college town where she grew up was showcased on the cover of *Life* magazine and in the world media following the shootings at Kent State in 1970. From that point on her worldview began to shift.

She taught school, because that's what women do. Circumstance forced her to change her career and join the corporate world, albeit still following a more traditional role. While there she began to take advantage of opportunities for breaking the mold. And, just as she began to come into her own, life took her to a college town, where she became the Professor's Wife.

But her spirit was no longer willing to be held in check by cultural expectations. She landed a job at the university, doors began to open, and suddenly there were many opportunities for *making things happen*. She caused change to happen in technology and business, became known for her stance on women's issues, and created a women's mentoring program, which is still going strong more than a decade later. Soon her spouse became *the husband of*; she grinned inwardly and never looked back.

And then her world turned upside down. She became a widow, and while marooned in the grief, she ultimately discovered a new, stronger, more confident self. And so she set about helping other women to recognize these traits in themselves.

One thing led to another and she retired from a job she loved to the great expanse of unnamed possibilities. Challenging herself to a Vision Quest, her life purpose became clear: assisting other women with their personal growth by shining a light on their inner strength and discovering ways to honor the gifts they have been given. Seeking the appropriate skills and credentialing, she became a student yet again, and proudly holds the Certified Professional Co-active* Coach (CPCC) standing.

Robin continues to enable women to find their voice and their innate power through her blog, workshops, life coaching, and publications. She finds the most joy in working 1-on-1 with women who want something *more* in their lives, who long to reintroduce *fun* and *passion* into their vocabulary and who hunger to reclaim the feeling of being deliciously alive.

She has a special place in her heart for those who:

> ➤ need a gentle nudge to manifest their innate gifts
> ➤ are ready to wholeheartedly engage life, on their terms
> ➤ believe they can make a difference in the world
> ➤ restore their inner peace in Mother Nature
> ➤ love cats (OK, and dogs, too), sensuous tea, dark chocolate and an occasional glass of really good wine.

Contact her at robin@chrysalislifecoach.com or learn more at chrysalislifecoach.com.

---

* *Coach and client take an equal responsibility for the relationship: the client sets the agenda; the coach creates a framework for personal growth, enabling the client to discover her own solutions.*

About the Designer

MISTY WILT
Owner + Designer • Misty Wilt Graphic Design LLC
www.mistywilt.com

Misty's life has always been inspired and motivated by color, shape, and texture. An accomplished jewelry designer and painter, as well as an award-winning graphic designer, Misty earned her BFA in Graphic Design at the prestigious Moore College of Art and Design in Philadelphia. She shares her work at regional exhibitions and works with budding artists at her alma mater whenever she can.

As an intern at Bowhaus Design Group in Philadelphia, Misty honed many of the skills that made her a successful graphic designer for Snavely Associates, a nationally focused communications firm, where Misty worked for nine years before launching Misty Wilt Graphic Design in 2011.

Reviewers' Comments

"Robin Anderson reveals her passion to empower other women by starting with the image of a burning ember that needs and deserves to be fanned into a life-warming flame within every woman. This reflects her journey and work with women over the last 25 years. And this *is* a book for women. From the nonstop coaching content and workbook-style approach to self-revelation, to the artistry of the words on the page, this book sings out the Call to every woman's (and man's, for that matter!) yearning to be who they are deep inside. The message is clear—the power of your passion isn't lost, it must be reclaimed! Anderson has no problem helping the reader reclaim parts that have been given away by time and convention. Thus helping everyone to remember his or her lost power.

This is an enormously helpful and fun workbook for counselors, too. *Reclaim Your Power!* is a surefire way to help and encourage clients to stay on task and get results where and when they are needed. A counselor could, with the aid of this workbook, easily assist their client to nurture the small ember of their heart, so hungry for air, into a roaring life-giving fire—and passionately live the life that is uniquely one's one."

—Beth A. Bollinger, MD, *Psychiatrist*

This book is contagious magic: a beautifully encouraging journey of self-empowerment, generously filled with insightful exercises that were so enticing I found myself having fun, getting lost in them, and emerging with a desire to embrace my power. Robin Anderson's voice is personal and warm; she shares her story with clarity and acceptance.

I went away not feeling pressured but inspired. I recommend this to all who are ready to live the life waiting for them.

—Jill Badonsky, *Founder of Kaizen-Muse Creativity Coaching, Author of Awe-manac, www.themuseisin.com*

Reclaim Your Power! provides a clearly written guide for women in search of their own authentic expression. Robin Anderson—having transformed herself—provides this book as the ultimate pay it forward gesture. She offers both the wise and loving voice of experience right alongside the voice that just dares you to begin anew. Any woman longing to banish the old inner guard in favor of the unbridled life will appreciate this clearly articulated, yet warm, workbook.

— Stephanie Yost Mentzell, *Certified Professional Co-Active Coach, www.thewholelifecoach and Creative Director of www.gumtreegrowth.com*

"It is a given that most self-help books be based on the premise that the reader is terribly flawed and must fix herself. Instead, Robin Anderson says, "Personal amnesia prevents us from remembering what we really want in our lives and what we truly believe." In *Reclaim Your Power!*, Anderson shows women how to rediscover, celebrate and use the power within them to become the women they were meant to be. In her engaging, conversational style, Anderson provides a safe environment along with tools for self-discovery. This wonderful book is positive, sensible, and truly helpful."

—Claudia Limbert, *President Emerita, Mississippi University for Women*

"This book provides a glimpse into Robin Anderson's gifts as a powerful coach and guide. *Reclaim Your Power!* offers a simple and effective model for making change in your life—change that moves you, at the pace you choose—toward the powerful and courageous person you are meant to be.

—Linda Gottschalk, *Senior Director of Global Talent Management, Research in Motion*

Robin Anderson's *Reclaim Your Power!* is a user-friendly guide to stepping up the game of full living. While one could easily read it in its entirety in a few short hours, they would miss the entire point. The good stuff isn't totally in the author's words. Readers are invited, through rigorous inquiry and practical exercises, to become co-authors and write their own stories of taking back their power. While I can't speak from a women's perspective, I wholeheartedly believe that digging into *Reclaim Your Power!* is not for the faint of heart. It's a workbook only for those serious about enjoying all life has to offer.

—Ken Mossman, PCC, CPCC, *Coaches Training Institute faculty member, owner of Cirrus Leadership*

Robin Anderson's book is such a breath of fresh air. We all deeply desire to reclaim our power and Anderson presents a great tool to make that happen. *Reclaim Your Power!* offers an encouraging place for women to make the necessary changes they yearn for. I so appreciated that she shows how to do it with a perfect combination of both taking action and sometimes just being. And, the anecdotes are perfect for knowing that there are others out there who have experienced the same things. Thank you, Robin, for giving us this awesome resource to reclaim our power once again.

—Kim Clausen, *Ready2Go Marketing Solutions, Inc., Broomfield, CO*

Notes

Please use the following pages to write your notes.

> "It's time to start living the
> life you've imagined."
> —Henry James

"Only as high as I reach can I grow,
Only as far as I seek can I go,
Only as deep as I look can I see,
Only as much as I dream can I be."

—**Karen Ravn**

"Life begins at the end of your comfort zone."

—**Neale David Walsh**

"Doubt yourself and you doubt everything you see. Judge yourself and you see judges everywhere. But if you listen to the sound of your own voice, you can rise above doubt and judgment. And you can see forever."

—Nancy Lopez

> "There's no crystal ball. The
> magic... is inside you."
> —Dolly Parton

"The most common way people give up their power is by thinking they don't have any." Alice Walker

"When you doubt your power, you give power to your doubt."

—HONORE DE BALZAC

"If I felt it was the right thing to do, I was for it regardless of the possible outcome."
—*Golda Meir*

"You gain strength, courage, and confidence by every experience in which you really stop to look fear in the face. You must do the thing which you think you cannot do."

—Eleanor Roosevelt